JIMMY BUFFETT

A Little Golden Book® Biography

By Donna Rocco • Illustrated by Tim Jessell

Golden Books
An imprint of Random House Children's Books
A division of Penguin Random House LLC
1745 Broadway, New York, NY 10019
penguinrandomhouse.com
rhcbooks.com

Library of Congress Control Number: 2025933359
ISBN 979-8-217-11654-6 (trade) — ISBN 979-8-217-11655-3 (ebook)
Manufactured in the United States of America
10 9 8 7 6 5 4 3 2
The authorized representative in the EU for product safety and compliance is Penguin Random House Ireland, Morrison Chambers, 32 Nassau Street, Dublin D02 YH68, Ireland.
https://eu-contact.penguin.ie

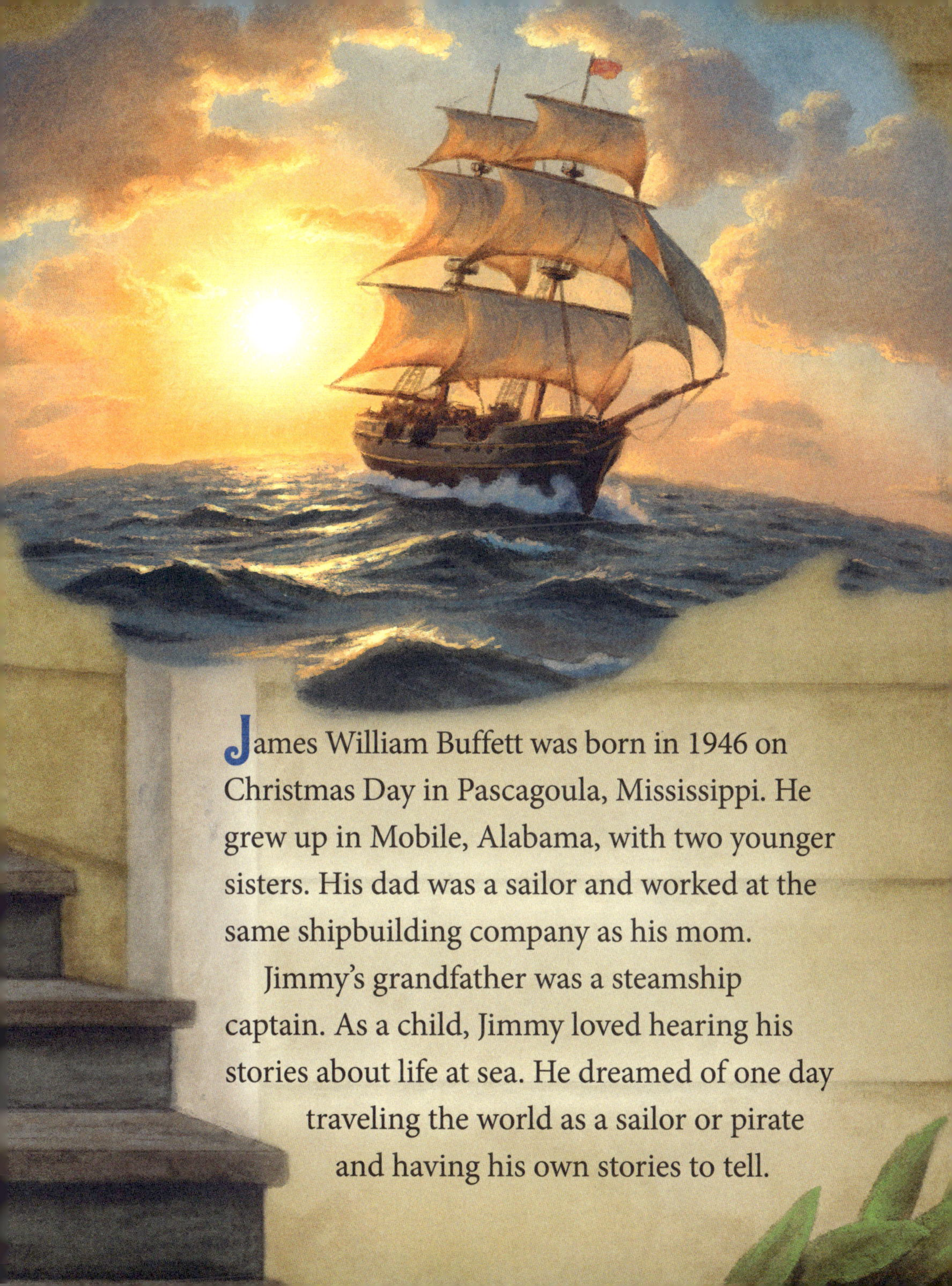

James William Buffett was born in 1946 on Christmas Day in Pascagoula, Mississippi. He grew up in Mobile, Alabama, with two younger sisters. His dad was a sailor and worked at the same shipbuilding company as his mom.

Jimmy's grandfather was a steamship captain. As a child, Jimmy loved hearing his stories about life at sea. He dreamed of one day traveling the world as a sailor or pirate and having his own stories to tell.

When Jimmy was little, he spent a lot of time exploring the Gulf Coast seashore. He fished, swam, and went sailing with his family. But one thing that could get him indoors was his grandmother's cooking, especially her gumbo!

Jimmy's mother wrote poetry and shared her love of reading with her children. Jimmy enjoyed reading adventure books about heroes and crooks. One of his favorite writers was Mark Twain.

Jimmy loved music, too. He played records on his family's Victrola and listened to songs on the radio. Some of his favorite singers were Elvis Presley and the New Orleans rhythm and blues musicians Allen Toussaint and Clarence "Frogman" Henry.

In high school, Jimmy was an altar boy, played trombone in the school band, and was a member of the varsity cheerleading team.

Jimmy went to college at Auburn University. There, he met a classmate who showed him how to play three chords on the guitar. Jimmy was hooked! He spent hours practicing. His grades began to slip, and he had to leave school.

He later transferred to the University of Southern Mississippi. Jimmy began playing guitar for audiences on campus. During one show, a student named Greg "Fingers" Taylor asked if he could play harmonica for a few songs. The two became friends and continued to play music together.

After college, Jimmy moved to the French Quarter in New Orleans. He played his guitar on the street for tips. He also joined a cover band and performed at local popular clubs. Soon, he started writing his own songs, too.

In 1970, Jimmy got a job as a reporter for a music magazine in Nashville. When he wasn't working, he was trying to get his songs heard by local record companies. His dream was to make it big as a musician.

It wasn't long before a record executive heard a song he liked called "The Captain and the Kid," which Jimmy wrote for his grandfather. He offered Jimmy a contract. His first album, *Down to Earth*, came out in 1970, but it didn't sell many copies.

One day, Jimmy and his friend country singer Jerry Jeff Walker decided to take a road trip. They piled into Jerry's 1947 Packard sedan, nicknamed the Flying Lady, and drove down the A1A highway from Miami to Key West—the southernmost city in the United States.

When they arrived in Key West, Jimmy marveled at the palm trees, water, and warm breezes. On their first night, they went to Mallory Square to watch the sun set into the Gulf of Mexico. Large crowds of people had gathered there to see the day's light turn to night.

Jimmy loved everything about the tropical island and decided to begin a new life there. He wrote songs inspired by the faces and places in Key West and performed at local clubs and cafés. One of the first songs he wrote was called "I Have Found Me a Home."

In 1971, Jimmy met Jane Slagsvol when she was vacationing on the island. Jimmy and Jane went to the beach together and spent time riding around in his green pickup truck. He played his music for her, too. Soon, they fell in love.

Jimmy released the album *A White Sport Coat and a Pink Crustacean* in 1973. It was his first record to make it onto the music charts. It was also the first time Jimmy played with some musicians who would later be in his backup group, the Coral Reefer Band, including college friend Fingers Taylor on harmonica.

The next year, the album *Living and Dying in ¾ Time* came out. "Come Monday," a song he wrote for Jane, became Jimmy's first big hit.

In 1977, Jimmy wrote a song that would change his life forever. He started writing "Margaritaville" when he was visiting Austin, Texas, and finished it while stuck in traffic on the Seven Mile Bridge on his way home to Key West. The song told the story of a man enjoying life in a beach town. It was the beginning of the laid-back island sound that Jimmy would become known for.

"Margaritaville" sold a million copies and became Jimmy's first top-ten song. His years of hard work had paid off!

Later that year, Jimmy and Jane got married in Redstone, Colorado. The Eagles, a popular country rock band, played at their wedding.

Together they would raise three kids, Savannah Jane, Sarah Delaney, and Cameron Marley.

Jimmy and the Coral Reefer Band toured all over the country and performed more than a hundred concerts each year. The shows were always fun, with the excited crowd singing along to their favorite tunes like "Cheeseburger in Paradise," "Fins," and of course "Margaritaville."

Jimmy's fans were called Parrotheads because of the colorful Hawaiian shirts, grass skirts, pirate hats, and parrot feathers they wore to each concert. Children of Parrotheads were called Parakeets.

When he wasn't writing songs or touring, Jimmy enjoyed surfing, flying planes, and spending time with his family. He wrote many books, including two children's books with his daughter Savannah Jane. And Jimmy loved playing with his dogs!

He also supported charities and did good deeds. He helped start the Save the Manatee Club and created Singing for Change, an organization that raises money to help people make a difference in their communities.

Jimmy Buffett died on September 1, 2023. Like his grandfather's stories and the books he read as a kid, Jimmy's life had been full of adventure. He traveled the world and sang for his fans for over fifty years. His songs taught us to find joy in life, to not give up on our dreams, and most of all, to have fun.

Parrotheads will keep the party going and continue to celebrate Jimmy's music for years to come.